CONTENTS

INTERVIEWS

STORIES AND ESSAYS

TRENDS

BOOK REVIEW

World Inkers Monthly Magazine

Editor: Dustin Pickering

ISBN: 9798808385436

SPECIAL FEATURES

POETRY

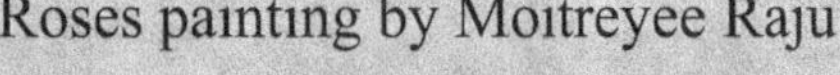

Roses painting by Moitreyee Raju

WHAT IF THE GODS ARE DAMN FOOLS?

From the Editor's Desk

Welcome to the special International Women's Month edition!

I've thought a lot about love, beauty, and why we love who we do and what factors into that concern. I have no answers. Many beautiful people exist and are attractive, but how many can one love? Is beauty the real hallmark or do energies coalesce into some harmonious being of their own? Why then unreciprocated love? The questions are endless. It seems Love just bounces around as it sees fit like a drunk lunatic marching amongst stars. If stars are diamonds on a table, Love must knock them to the floor in protest. But doth He protest too much? It's a truly eccentric question, though. Why love and why love prevails? Britney Spears is beautiful but I don't develop affectionate love for her. So beauty isn't the end all here. There must be some filial tie, some marked display of courage, some bond outside spacetime constraints that universalizes harmony between humankind's rage fits. Passion consumes and liquidates the soul, giving birth to room for new things born afresh through the solemn mound of death and dearth.

The reason poets write is to engage with that passion through conceptual language. As Heidegger is noted to have suggested, language is the essence of our being and not our creation. Something within the human mind desires to express its lowly passions through language. We are anxious creatures and that anxiety is eased by discussion, conversation and writing. Writing is conveyed into permanence. What more could Love be than permanence? What makes a great writer the sustained influence they become? Perhaps as Emily Dickinson wrote, "Tis the majority in all prevail." There are no universal rules determining the greatness of a writer although they must assume the banners of tradition to appeal to the masses and convey meaning in ways that are construed popularly in the imagination.

-From World Inkers 2022 Symposium on Poetry and Healing

Available from the publisher

finishinglinepress.com

$19.99

R. W. Haynes

Heidegger Looks at the Moon

These are wonderful poems. In the best poetic tradition, they come alive and prod memories through elegant allusions to classical mythology, literature, and popular culture. Thinkers like Heidegger, of course, pop singers like Sam the Sham, writers like Harry Crews, common folk like Big Jake, as well as literary, classical, biblical and historical characters, populate the world found here. R.W. Haynes' masterful command of language and poetic forms inspires the reader to come on board and enjoy the ride, and we are the richer for traveling along with the poet to Waco or Ft. Stockton, crossing the Rio Grande with Charon, and visiting imagined pasts or literary spaces with Oswald Alving or Chaucer.

Norma Elia Cantú,

Norine R. and T. Frank Murchison Professor of the Humanities, Trinity University, author of *Canícula* and numerous other works of prose and poetry.

THE SEASON OF POETS- BOOK REVIEW

Rozalia Aleksandrova

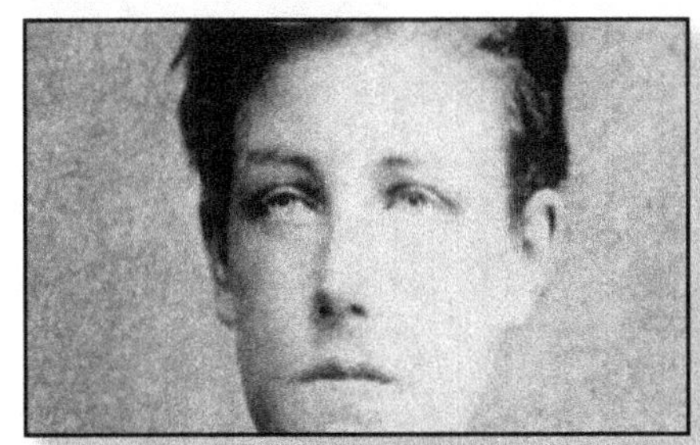

The challenges of the thirties of the Third Millennium are also facing Poetry. These are factors that act on a spiritual, physical, emotional and intellectual level. They affect values and established frameworks in global society. Waves of negative emotions swirl in all directions of the horizontal and vertical of human and earthly society. Today the world is headed to the counterpoint of the metaphor Life. It looks like that.

And, unexpectedly, negative emotions and events are tamed in the new bright movement of poetic society around the world. He already has it. Here and now! Poetry invisibly stabilizes and neutralizes chaotic manifestations. Because She is clothed in the words of the Energy of creation. True Poetry is not a reflection of visible reality. It is the warm hand of the Creator, extended to people in this significant moment through the word.

What are the words in poetry that are important to man? Words that we call good. Words that make us rejoice, believe and hope. To laugh, to understand and to love. They give us answers to existential questions. Moreover, in Poetry there are answers that are given with very few words, or sometimes without words.

Poets are engaged in the eternal questions of existence by raising and landing thought, through questions and answers that often change the perspective of social prejudice. Seen through the prism of eternal present time. Through purity and harmony.

Now is the season of poets!

They are torches of spiritual development. They are called to justify God's blessing on people. Poetic society at this time can be called global without any additions and injected self-confidence. The reason for this are the literary sites, anthologies, almanacs published in Europe and around the world. The flow of public events - poetry festivals, premieres and newly published books of poetry - seems to race against time. Among them the activity of the literary sites is especially fruitful and important.

One such site, which can be called a representative sample of a successful contemporary poetic site, is Atunis Galaxy Poetry. Its publisher is the great poet Agron Shele (Albania - Belgium). Every year, in collaboration with the Dutch publishing house Demer Press, led by the poet Hannie Rouweler, Agron Shele creates an anthology that includes works by poets from around the world.

This year's anthology "Atunis Galaxy Anthology 2022" is an exquisite edition in red, white and light gray. And inside are collected works of 167 poets from around the globe. When one turns its pages, one understands that here Poetry has done its universal role - to give a cure for the pains of the soul, to strengthen the body and to help readers to look at the experiences of poets as in their own mirror. Diverse in style, despite the English language framework, this anthology holds the full range of human emotions and thoughts: from the wild horses of imagination and enthusiasm to the calm strength and depth of the wise gaze of our contemporaries.

Poetry as an essence and a sacred message is apolitical. This can be seen in the selection of verses made by the compiler Agron Shele. The only policy of Poetry is to bring people together in the name of Goodness, Harmony, Beauty and Love.
In a slightly more specific plan, I will focus on some images that thematically unite the authors.

The first of them is the image of the Rose, which is a symbol of inner purity. With it, poets discover the world of beauty and perfection we strive for.

The image of the Way is present even in verses that do not contain this sacred word. There are two directions in the interpretations of this topic: the human and the divine way.

One subtopic of the above is the search for a direct conversation with God. And the gratitude of our contemporaries for the opportunity to be here on Earth at this very moment.
The theme of Love as the eternal engine of Life is recreated in all its aspects.

A special beauty is contained in the theme of the Contemplation of magical reality. And in the eyes of the poet it is only such.

How the doors of Happiness are unlocked - the creators of the word know how to express it in a few but precise words.

In this poetic anthology there are many verses that speak of Joy as a life-affirming force and Joy as a building material for the present and future of mankind.

A concrete but also charismatic image is that of the Wind. The wind of Hope, of parting with difficulties, of Freedom to be a real person.
The image of Silence is, perhaps, the greatest challenge for the reader. From the silence of loneliness to the understanding of this mighty force as a unifying island of All created and uncreated.

Often poets look at the sky. Because their gaze is always an open door to true values, to sacred truths. They have the ability to reshape times and spaces with words, to be human and to become messengers. Visible and invisible. To transform everyday life into their incredibly beautiful mind and world. Thus the warmth of their feelings and thoughts poured out on the white sheets of the anthology.

This process, which is observed in the anthology, is parallel to the processes that move humanity. The avalanche-like unification of poets from all over the world is indicative of the development of human society. A sign that people need beauty and harmony, love and support not in some distant future, but now. Literary anthologies, sites and forums become an arena of new ideas, friendships and love, blessed and supported by the power of Evolution - the ubiquitous law of human and cosmic development.

Woman and Raven by Cynthia Yachtman

WOMEN
Eva Petropoulou Lianou

An eternal flame
A birth that embrace the whole earth with feelings.
Since a woman came to this planet
Curiousity came with her

Look at Eva in the paradise
She always wanted to know
More about her environment
Her friends
Her husband

Is the curiosity the only thing that women have?
No, jealousy and envy
Beauty and luxury
Kindness and generosity
But who ever say that can understand the women?!
Nobody

Even the women themselves
They cannot understand eachother
Is a jungle out there
And often they fight for a man, for a car, for a dress,
for a pair of shoes ..

But there are women and women
Some women are so generous and kind
They have the light inside them
They have self respect
They are helping friends, non friends
Strangers
Stray dogs
They are like Angel s in this big dark world

A secret
If you find a woman like that
Keep her close to your heart.

Eva Petropoulou Lianou is an ambassador for World Inkers Network.

ADVERTISEMENT

Q & A with AMY FERRIS

Screenwriter, anthologist, author

Thank you for taking the time to speak with World Inkers Monthly Magazine concerning depression. Also, congratulations on being nominated as one of 2022's Women of the Year. Can you tell us about your own struggles with depression and why de-stigmatizing the illness is important?

My struggles began when I was a young girl. Felt very isolated and lonely. I was different; I didn't love sports, I wasn't a tag-along type of girl. I felt very left out. Depression kind of crept in at a young age. I tried suicide when I was 14/15 and luckily I failed at that one attempt. Depression should be treated like any and all diseases. It must be de-stigmatized.

Depression is seen sometimes as laziness or inability to cope with life issues. How do you feel about such criticisms and have you faced them yourself? How do you personally overcome the soul-draining aspect of the illness?

I don't have it as bad as many. I take my meds. They calm me down. But for folks who truly can't be out in the world… that's horribly scary. And the world is scary. Do, it's a double-edged sword sometimes. I know for my self that ART saves me. Creating. Writing. Being a part of a creative environment. Art truly saves lives. It keeps us active in beauty.

What role has artistic purpose played in your struggle? Has depression been alleviated by artistic works? I find sometimes I face depression and energy lags after a massive creative project.

I'm a writer and I try desperately to put all that energy into words. Into helping/mentoring others.

What resources are available for sufferers to learn more about depression and how to deal constructively with its harsh effects?

NAMI has some extraordinary resources.
THIS is MY Brave is absolutely magnificent and has been a lifeline for mental health issues.
Depressed Cake Shop is extraordinary.

How do you personally assist others living with depression as a sufferer yourself? What are positive ways we can bridge understandings between sufferers and non-sufferers? How common is mental illness in the general population, and why do you think it is more common than we admit?

This is a hard question. I try, through my writing, to inspire and encourage and lift other folks up who struggle in their sorrow and pain and I do that through my writing. Whether it's a post a day on FaceBook or through essays or speaking up. When we feel we're not alone in the world… we feel less afraid. We feel like we have a community. Depression does not discriminate one bit. It doean't care what color you are or what your bank account looks like. The best we can do, is SHARE our Stories. Share them so others don't feel alone. Share, talk, write… and keep on doing that.

***

RESOURCES

https://www.nami.org/Home

https://thisismybrave.org/

https://depressedcakeshop.org/

Q & A with LEAH HUETE DE MAINES

Publisher, poet, entrepreneur

Since you began Finishing Line Press, what have been some highlights in publishing for you? Why did you start publishing and what skills and education helped you develop the business?

Finishing Line Press is home to many award-winning authors, including Susanna Rich, author of the FLP chapbook The Drive Home. Some of the poems from Rich's collection were included in the documentary film Cobb Field: A Day in the Ballpark. Susanna Rich and Craig Lindvahl were nominated for a Mid-America Emmy Award in the category "Writers/Program" for the film. Susanna was kind enough to invite me to attend the Emmy Awards. It was an amazing evening, and a great honor to have a Finishing Line Press book connected to the project. Another highlight in my FLP career was when Ilene Starger, author of the FLP chapbook Lethe, Postponed had the some of the poems from the book set to music by composer Eric Shimelonis, and performed by Academy Award and Golden Globe winner F. Murray Abraham at Carnegie Hall in New York City to a full house. In addition to these exciting events, many of our authors have won, or have been finalists in, prestigious book awards such as the Massachusetts Book Awards, the Oklahoma Book Award, the Northeastern Minnesota Book Award, the Kentucky Literary Award, and the Next Generation Indie Book Awards, among many others.

Does Finishing Line Press focus mostly on women? How do you select them for publishing? Your wide catalogue is impressive!

Finishing Line Press is the home of the New Women's Voices Chapbook Competition. However, our publishing focus is not solely on women. We strive to publish the best voices in poetry and fiction regardless of one's gender. We select our authors based on the quality of their work.

Thank you so much for the fine work you do. In conclusion, why did you select literature as your focus? What else do you do artistically to relax?

Publishing poetry has long been a passion of mine. It has been a learning process too. It has been important for me to keep up with the trends in publishing. When FLP started back in 1998 social media was not a thing. Now, over two decades later, social media has become a particularly important part of keeping connected with our authors, and future authors. We utilize social media to promote all of our new books, and to give our authors exposure.

ARTIST:

Lavanya Yadav

Student, 10th Class

Janki Devi Public School

Jaipur, India

A WOMAN FROM THE BALKANS

Nermina Subašić

When you are born in the Balkans,

and besides, you're just a woman,

you curse yourself,

because no one is lucky there.

The woman there is a slave in the house,

who has no rights,

all my life to suffer,

she washes, cooks, cleans the house.

It's always been that way here,

and the woman does not raise her voice,

It's not easy for anyone here,

but the woman is even lower.

Don't live like that anymore,

raise your head up,

everything is upside down here,

because women are to be loved.

Woman is the ornament of the world,

even here in the Balkans,

keep a woman like a flower,

like an unharvested rose.

Photo of Nermina Subašić

Nermina Subašić, 1998 born in Tuzla, Bosnia and Herzegovina. Final year student of the Faculty of Dentistry Sarajevo. She published the novel "Crime and Forgiveness", which was named the best debut novel in 2016. Winner of Bosnian and international literary awards.

PAULINE JOHNSON: A Mohawk Princess Poet
by W. Ruth Kozak

If you visit my city, Vancouver, British Columbia, Canada, you are sure to spend some time in one of Vancouver's unique tourist attractions, Stanley Park. The park covers 404.9 hectares (1,000 acres) of rainforest and is the largest city park in North America. It was named for Lord Stanley, 16th Earl of Derby who became Governor General of Canada. Stanley Park was first opened as a public recreation area in 1887. The park, which is located at the western entrance to Vancouver's harbour, was originally settled by the Coast Salish people. It was their hunting and gathering ground and became the favorite haunt of an Indian princess/poet, Pauline Johnson, the first Native Indian to be published in Canada. Her book *"The White Wampum"* gained her high literary standing.

Born March 10, 1861 on her father's estate "Chiefswood" on the Six Nations Indian Reserve near Brantford, Ontario, Pauline was the youngest child of G.H.M. Johnson, head Chief of the Six Nations and his English wife Emily S. Howells. Her Indian name was *Tekahionwake*. She was considered a "princess" because her father was the scion of 50 noble families which composed the historical confederation founded by Hiawatha, a noble chief made famous in a poem by Alfred, Lord Tennyson. It was known as the Brotherhood of the Five Nations.

Pauline's education was meagre — a nursery governess for two years, attendance at a Native Canadian day school, and two finishing years at the Brantford Central School — but she was well educated in the School of Nature. With her voracious reading, retentive memory, and keen mind, Pauline acquired a wide knowledge of literature, especially poetry. Before she was twelve, she had read all the classics. Her fiest poems were published in New York and Toronto. By the time she was in her 20's she became known for her public appearances and poetry readings, traveling from the Atlantic to the Pacific coasts of Canada. She also made several trips to England to perform and was presented to the Queen. She performed in dance halls across the country often clad in a buckskin outfit and a bear claw necklace to represent her Mohawk heritage and then later in the performance she'd change into a silk evening gown honoring her British ancestry.

Much of Johnson's poetry focused on her cultural back-ground. In *A Cry From an Indian Wife* she wrote:

"Go forth, nor bend to greed of white man's hands.
By right, by birth, we Indians own these lands,
Though starved, crushed, plundered,
Lies our nation low;
Perhaps the white man's God has willed it so."

Pauline Johnson made many trips to the west coast, eventually settling in Vancouver. She spent much of her time in Stanley Park. She was an ardent canoeist and a great lover of nature and wrote many poems about the park.

As I enter the Park, I cross under the causeway and take the path to Lost Lagoon. Originally part of Coal Harbour, it was a tidal basin where Indians dug clams. In the early days, visitors to the park had to pick their way over a large log anchored in the mud flats until eventually wooden bridge was built. The causeway, constructed of earth, ashes and street-sweepings, was built in 1888. Pauline Johnson loved to paddle her canoe here. She named this tidal pool "Lost Lagoon" because of the way it emptied when the tide ebbed, and she wrote:

"O! lure of the lost Lagoon/ I dream tonight my paddle blurs/ The purple shade when the seaweed stirs/ I hear the call of the singing firs/ In the hush of the golden moon."

The native name for Lost Lagoon is "Chul-Wah-Ulch" which means "a bog which is dry when the tide is out" Once there were Indian dwellings on the north side of the lagoon. Now, trumpeter swans, mute swans, duck families and grey herons make their home on the lagoon.

As I walk along the lagoon, I can feel Pauline's presence and recall her poem about the Lagoon:

It is dusk on the Lost Lagoon,
And we two dreaming the dusk away,
Beneath the drift of a twilight grey-
Beneath the drowse of an ending day
And the curve of a golden moon –"

I follow the path to the end of the Lagoon to the seawall at Second Beach. As I walk along the seawall I come to another place that Pauline Johnson liked to visit in the park —Siwash Rock *"where the twining roadway branches in two".* This monument of nature stands as a reminder to the Squamish people of one man who lived a good life. The tall pinnacle of rock that rises just off the shore represents *Skalsh,* a warrior who was turned into stone by *Q'Uas the Transformer* as a reward for his unselfishness. It is one of the best known legends about a young Indian who was about to become a father and decided to swim in the waters of English Bay to purify himself so his new-born son could start life free of his father's sins. The gods made Sklash immortal by turning him into a pinnacle of rock. Two smaller rocks representing his wife and son stand in the woods overlooking Siwash Rock.

Pauline Johnson died in Vancouver at the age of 53, on March 7, 1913. The hardships of travel in those days had taken a toll on her health and in the latter years of her life this remarkable woman, known to her friends as 'a beloved vagabond' became an invalid. The last thing she wrote was her will, nine days before her death at 53, in which she requested no public mourning, no tombstone or monument. But a huge funeral was held with hundreds of people in the streets to honor her. Her will and ashes were lost for 43 years before they were found in the vault of a Vancouver law firm. Her ashes and two of her books *Legends of Vancouver* and *Flint and Feather* were eventually buried near Siwash Rock. In 1922 the Women's Canadian Club of Vancouver erected a monument in her honour.

I visit the cairn in a cedar grove at Prospect Point near the Stanley Park Tearoom. It's a simple relief carved out of a large piece of natural rock, where water flows from the rocks into a small hollow pool at its base. This day, someone has left a bouquet of flowers in her memory. I pause, engulfed in the silence of the tall cedars that surround the shrine, and pay homage to this remarkable woman whose beautiful poetry has given such a special meaning to Stanley Park.

* * *

PAULINE JOHNSON'S BIO:

http://en.wikipedia.org/wiki/Pauline_Johnson

http://digital.library.upenn.edu/women/garvin/poets/johnson.html

BOOKS

http://www.amazon.ca/Pauline-Johnson-Tekahionwake-Collected-Selected/dp/0802084974

http://www.goodminds.com/booksatom/E.-Pauline-Johnson-Tekahionwake-Collected-Poems-a.html

POETRY COLLECTIONS

http://www.poemhunter.com/emily-pauline-johnson-tekahionwake/

Photo by W. Ruth Kozak

Pauline Johnson from public domain

NO ONE TO LISTEN
Antara Roy Bhattacharjee

A woman, yes she is a woman indeed;
Whenever her heart cries out in pain.
There is no one to listen;
Her struggles and fears are misinterpreted in vain.

Quite often she is utterly repressed and depressed
She flutters and jolts
But finds none by her side to back her up once again.

She is a loving mother,caring daughter,affectionate sister,
an adorable wife a rocking friend.
If she is a single mother,
She receives raised eyebrows from many
for she is unwilling to mingle.

Tears roll down siliently within
There is no one to listen.

Somewhere, a girl of fifteen is married off to a man of fifty
To pay off the debts.
She cries out remorsefully
Is she a material who has been won on a bet?
But,there is no one to listen.

Somewhere in a family, instead of rejoicing, few exchange sullen glances
For the first child born is a daughter,
Thinking of who will carry forward this patriarchy further.
Have we gone back to the medieval?
But,There is no one to listen.

The inner musings of a woman can hardly be read and deciphered;
Shall it always remain unheard?
Her journey from birth till death she is only there to please everyone;
Why such legacy carries on for ages!
Its time to end this and bring true happiness and smile on all faces.

Antara Roy Bhattacharjee is a young vibrant writer from Kolkata, West Bengal. She has a PG Diploma in Journalism and Mass-communication from Jadavpur University (J.U) along with a Masters in English literature from IGNO. She has taken up teaching as her profession. Poetry writing is her passion. Recently her book on poems "Percipience poetry to perceive" has been published by BFC Publications Private Limited, across various online platforms like Amazon Kindle, Amazon.com. She has also completed her senior diploma in Hindustani Classical music.

Domestic Violence against Women during the Pandemic in India

Debajyoti Gupta

Abstract

Domestic violence, a prevalent problem in India, saw an increase during the lockdown imposed to contain the spread of COVID-19. Findings reveal that sources of motivation in domestic violence perpetrators during the lockdown were alcohol and unemployment however there are also many factors for the reason of domestic violence against women in the form of sexual assets, emotional violence, Dowry, etc I have also tries to find out the causes of this violence and why it has been hidden during the pandemic.

Keywords- Factors, spread, pandemic, problem, reason.

Introduction

Violence against women and girls is regarded as a global pandemic that affects one in every three women across their lifetime. An estimated 736 million women become victims of intimate partner violence or non-partner sexual violence, or both, at least once in their life.

The international community has long acknowledged this problem. In 1995, the Beijing Declaration and Platform for Action called for the elimination of violence against women. A decade later, in 2015, the UN adopted the 2030 Agenda for Sustainable Development which included a global target to eliminate "all forms of violence against women and girls in public and private spheres. In 2016, the World Health Assembly Resolution 69.5 called for a global plan of action to strengthen the role of the health system within a national multisector response to address interpersonal violence, particularly against women and young girls. Despite all these, however, 49 countries have yet to adopt a formal policy on domestic violence.

Any aggressive act, abusive behaviour, or harassment in different forms between adults who are or have been intimate partners or family members, regardless of gender or sexuality, is considered domestic violence, it is committed by someone in the victim's domestic circle and they maintain a domestic relationship.

It is not just the physical violence or the visible injuries which are treated to be domestic violence but actions such as taking control over the spouse, sexual abuse, emotional abuse or isolation and coercion, threatening would all come under domestic violence. This is not just pertaining to an area, a city or a country this is a global topic that transcends national borders, socio-economic, educational, ethnic, and class divisions it is widely spread and strongly rooted.

Most of time it's the women who suffer either in their own house or in their in -laws' homes by intimate partners in various forms. United Nations report says that around 70% of women around the globe have suffered domestic violence at some point in their life.

Intimate partner abuse or domestic violence is most often caused by marital dispute or discord in a relationship. Studies have shown that domestic violence mostly happens in a family with low level income and low educational level, so in situations when a woman has a higher educational status, she tends to be less affected by such problems but few other studies have shown that women with higher educational qualification are abused more by their intimate partners. [1]

Research methods

My research is based on the secondary data which is collected for my study. I searched news articles on the Google search using certain keywords. These keywords were "domestic violence," "marital violence," "lockdown," "COVID-19," "corona virus," and "India."

Aim of the study

This study aims to provide a large-scale analysis of public discourse on women violence which occurred in India during the COVID-19 pandemic. The research questions are as follows: (1) what are the causes of Domestic violence during the pandemic (2) What are the cases of domestic violence? 3. Why the cases for domestic violence have been hidden during pandemic?

Causes of Domestic violence in the pandemic

It has been seen that the problem of domestic violence in India during the pandemic was for alcohol and unemployment.

(I) Alcohol - The relationship between alcohol and domestic violence is not something that emerged during COVID-19. Many studies concluded that alcohol does not cause domestic violence. Rather it is seen as a contributing factor towards the perpetration of domestic violence. The ban on alcohol does not mean that consumption also came to a halt. Many black-marketing and illegal purchase and sale of alcohol cases were reported.

(ii) Unemployment- Previous studies conducted in India highlighted the association between husband's unemployment and domestic violence. It has been found women whose husbands maintained stable employment were less likely to experience domestic violence. Countries across the world faced the employment crisis as COVID-19 affected the functioning of all kinds of businesses.

These are some of the causes that can be seen in India during the Pandemic but there is also other form of domestic violence such as:

1. Physical violence - The scope of physical domestic/intimate partner violence includes slapping, pushing, kicking, biting, hitting, throwing objects, strangling, beating, threatening with any form of weapon, or using a weapon.

2. Emotional violence - has been gaining more and more recognition in recent years as an incredibly common form of domestic violence. Psychological abuse can erode a woman's sense of self-worth and can be incredibly harmful to overall mental and physical wellbeing. Emotional/psychological abuse can include harassment; threats; verbal abuse such as name-calling, degradation and blaming; stalking; and isolation

3. Sexual assets - Domestic sexual assault is a form of domestic violence involving sexual/reproductive coercion and marital rape. Under Indian law, marital rape is not a crime, except during the period of marital separation of the partners

4. Honor killings - An honour killing is the practice wherein an individual is killed by one or more family member(s), because he or she is believed to have brought shame on the family. The shame may range from refusing to enter an arranged marriage, having sex outside marriage being in a relationship that is disapproved by the family, starting a divorce proceeding, or engaging in homosexual relations.

5. Dowry related death and abuse - In almost all Hindu families; the ritual of taking dowry has caused a serious problem. Newly married brides suffer domestic violence in the form of harassment, physical abuse or death when she is thought to have not brought enough dowries with marriage. Some cases end up in suicides by hanging, self-poisoning or by fire. In dowry deaths, the groom's family is the perpetrator of murder or suicide.

Dowry deaths in India are not limited to any specific religion, and it is found among   Hindus, Muslims, Sikhs and others. Some 80% of the total Dowry related crime found in the Hindu community followed by other Indian religions as giving Dowry is considered as an important ritual in the traditional Hindu marriage. Furthermore, in many parts of India the Ritual of Tilak *(Engagement)* done mostly in Hindu families is used by Groom's Family to Demand a huge sum of money. [2]

Cases of domestic violence in India during pandemic

In the case of domestic violence, mostly men are seen as predator. Though men also experience domestic violence but in societies where patriarchy prevails, domestic violence is usually associated with women as victims identified that offenders often want to put the least amount of effort to carry out the criminal activities such as travelling significantly less distance to find a target and choosing a target who is evident and proximate .This explains the rise in domestic violence cases during COVID-19, as home became the very space. A motivated offender now has to put in the least amount of effort to find its target.

On 22nd March 2020, the Prime Minister of India announced a nationwide lockdown for one day. This lockdown was subsequently extended for a week, then for 21 days and finally until 3rd May 2020 to contain the spread of COVID-19. Extended lockdown and other social distancing measures imposed to curb the pandemic made women more vulnerable to domestic violence. Women were fighting a shadow pandemic inside their homes.

National Commission for Women's (NCW) data showed that domestic violence complaints doubled after the nationwide lockdown were imposed in India. Some of the states in India such as Tamil Nadu and Bangalore have shown a number of cases on women violence during the pandemic.

In Tamil Nadu, Police reported an increase in domestic violence complaints. They received approximately 25 calls every day during the lockdown period and registered at least 40 such cases. In Bangalore, Police reported a spike in complaints from 10 calls to 25 calls every day from the victims of domestic violence .These data from different sources indicate that domestic violence incidents increased across the country during the lockdown. [3] Another cases in the north east India a girl was sexual harassed in her school by his teacher and after that the Police took necessary actions against the person.

Cases of Domestic violence has been hidden during the Pandemic

Restricted movement: The lockdown stopped women by preventing them from moving to safer places in cases of violence and abuse.

Handicapped mediums of communication: A Whatsapp number was launched by the National Commission for Women in India had a limited reach as only 38% of women in India own phones and fewer have an internet connection, making this platform difficult for the majority of women in the country.

Reduced contact with the natal family: Natal family is usually the first point of contact for the victim. They are not only essential in supporting the victim in filing a complaint but also facilitate filing of complaints to the police. The constant presence of the perpetrator made it difficult for the victims to contact their first respondent which ultimately stop them from reporting to institutionalised channels.

Unavailability of the formal support system: The machinery under the Protection of Women from Domestic Violence Act had not been identified as an essential service during the lockdown. Hence, the protection officers were not able to visit households of victims, NGOs were not able to have physical interactions with them and the police officers being at the frontline in our effort to tackle COVID-19 were overstretched to help victims effectively.

While the nationwide restrictions have been relaxed, various state and district level lockdowns are invoked every now and then, allowing the pandemic of domestic violence to sprout alongside. We must not count violence against women as an inevitable outcome of a crisis but improve the otherwise delayed policy implications to address the situation.

Conclusion

It can be seen that during this Pandemic we all have seen different type of situation where the world is effected by the problem of Covid 19 virus and in the other hand, some of the women are facing the problem of domestic violence and some of this cases are hidden due to non – proper communication with the officials due to lockdown and low network connection especially in the rural areas.

My study is not only restricted to strict and effective legal provisions to help these women but also to focus the attention of scholars and mental health professionals to study and design effective interventions so as to educate and prepare a gender equality that can shatter the existing power hierarchy based on gender, not only the government and law enforcement agencies but also the non-governmental organisations and the general public must come together to create conditions in which reaching out for help to make it easy.

References

1. Sindhu, Domestic Violence: the hidden pandemic. https://www.legalserviceindia.com/legal/article-7736-domestic-violence-the-hidden-pandemic.html.

2. Domestic violence against women, Wikipedia. https://en.wikipedia.org/wiki/Domestic_violence_in_India

3. Akshaya Krishnakumar and Shankey Verma (2021). Understanding Domestic Violence in India during COVID-19: a Routine Activity Approach. doi: 10.1007/s11417-020-09340-1

In the Image of God
Tali Cohen Shabtai

To whom will you imagine me and compare me to?

"For in his image he
created man."

As worded,
I am
called a man (Adam in Hebrew)
named after the earth (Adama in Hebrew)
why was I named as a man after the lowest
part of creation?
For that I am flattered. In any case
the sky is not achievable.

And yet at the same time as a man I am
treated upliftingly and exaltedly that the Torah gives
me
for the Creator of the World who chose
me in his image and in this passes over
my futility
in front of God? I relish
ironic statements like this,
but

as long as I don't know
the sight of God

It does not interest me
that it's possible to simulate a shape to its creator
like clay in the potter's hand
and allow me to reflect on
this paradox:

hence, God can
wear my bra
snort a cigarette and confront
the forlorn thoughts that
visit me
in Jerusalem – where
the divine revelation in the world
resides, so to speak.

And if I was created in God's image,
from here it is possible to compare with the parable
about a craftsman who with does the material
as he pleases,
for which it is called "matter in the hand of the creator"
but should I admire
that I
am in God's hands like the matter in the hand of the artist?

And more than that, it is said
that I was created in his image.
Of course not.

Tali Cohen Shabtai, born in Jerusalem, Israel, is a highly-esteemed international poet with works translated into many languages. She has authored three bilingual volumes of poetry, "Purple Diluted in a Black's Thick"(2007), "Protest" (2012) and "Nine Years From You"(2018). A fourth volume is forthcoming in 2022. Tali began writing poetry at the age of six. She lived for many years in Oslo, Norway, and the U.S.A. and her poems express both the spiritual and physical freedom paradox of exile. Her cosmopolitan vision is obvious in her writings. Tali is known in her country as a prominent poet with a unique narrative. As one commentator wrote: "She doesn't give herself easily, but is subject to her own rules."

WOMEN ARE ALWAYS POWERFUL
Monalisa Parida

- India

Being a woman means having a strong sense of identity, accepting your body as one that adapts and changes over time, being confident, and building up the people in your life. It means you have the wisdom to be grateful for what you have while still being hungry enough for growth.

Women's multiple roles........

As a daughter, a woman is traditionally responsible for taking care of her parents. As a wife, she is expected to serve her husband, preparing food, clothing and other personal needs. As a mother, she has to take care of the children and their needs, including education.

Women did tasks as important as those of men, managed their households, and were equals in daily life, but all public decisions were made by men. Men had specific obligations they were required to perform for their wives including the provision of clothing, food, and sexual relations.

Women play a very vital role in human progress and have a significant place in the society. They are not at all inferior to men. They are capable of sharing all the responsibilities of life. The main responsibility of a woman is to preserve the human race. Throughout history, the central role of women in society has ensured the stability, progress and long-term development of nations. Being a woman means being able to be powerful and assertive, yet kind at the same time.

The role of women in socio-political landscapes..........

Women's political participation is **a** fundamental prerequisite for gender equality and genuine democracy. Women have held the posts of president and prime minister in many countries, as well as chief ministers of various states.

Here is the name of few powerful name of women politicians.......

1. Angela Merkel

2. Christine Lagarde

3. Kamala Harris

4. Ursula von der Leyen

5. Nancy Pelosi

6. Kristalina Georgieva

7. Jacinda Ardern

8. Tsai Ing-Wen

9. Sheikh Hasina Wajed

10. Nirmala Sitharaman

11. Queen Elizabeth II

12. Erna Solberg

13. Simonetta Sommaruga

14. Elvira Nabiullina

15. Nicola Sturgeon

16. Yuriko Koike

17. Sophie Wilmes

18. Mette Frederiksen

19. Sri Mulyani Indrawati

20. Zuzana Caputova

21. Sanna Marin

22. Sahle-Work Zewde

23. Stacey Abrams

The role of women in Economic landscapes.....

The woman performs the role of wife, partner, organizer, administrator, director, re-creator, disburser, economist, mother, disciplinarian, teacher, health officer, artist and queen in the family at the same time. Apart from it, woman plays a key role in the socio-economic development of the society. Empowering more women to work, results in better growth of third-world economies. This is because women's economic empowerment, increases economic diversification, boosts productivity and income equality, resulting in other positive development outcomes. An economic developer is responsible for planning, designing, and implementing economic development strategies, as well as acting as a key liaison between public and private sectors and the community.

Amartya Sen has been called the "Mother Teresa" of Economics.

Katharine Eillis Coman was World's first Economics.

Here is the example of most popular women economists in the world......

1. Carmen M. Reinhart

2. Esther Duflo

3. Asli Demirguc-Kant

4. Janet Currie

5. Marianne Bertrand

6. Bronwyn Hughes Hall

7. Claudia Goldin

8. Serena Ng

9. Ellen R. McGrattan

10. Olivia S. Mitchell

In the words of Louisa May Alcott:

"When women are the advisor, the Lords of creation don't take the advice till they have persuaded themselves that it is just what they intended to do; then they act upon it and if it succeeds, they give the weaker vessel half the credit of it; if fails, they generously give herself the whole."

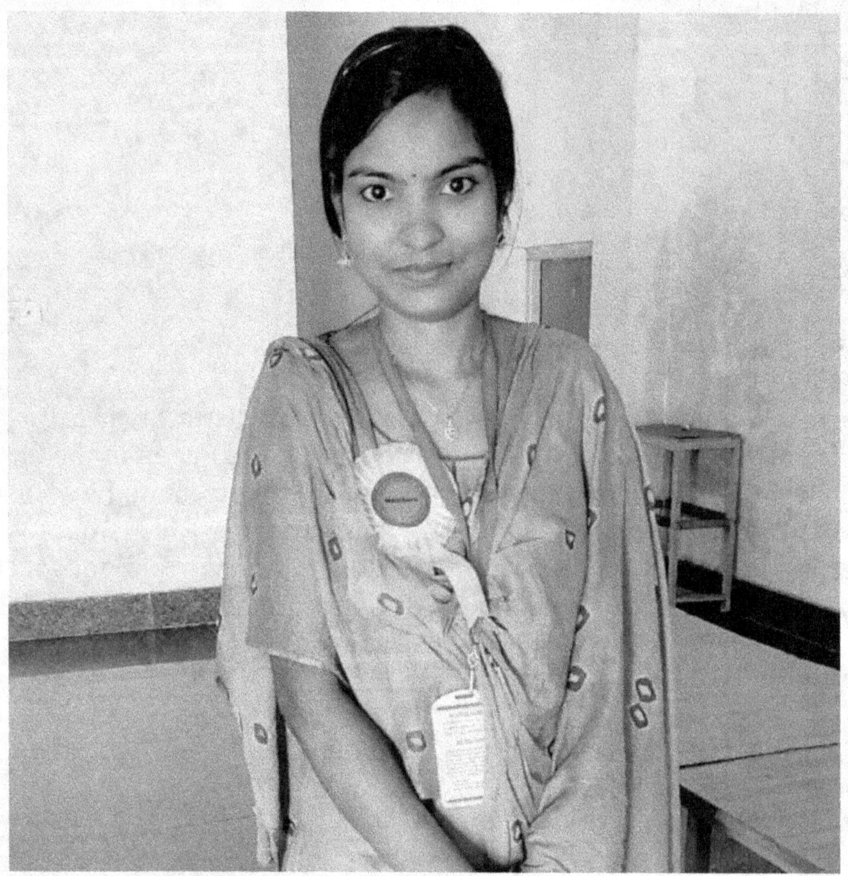

Monalisa Parida is from India, Odisha. She is a post graduate in English literature and a prolific poetess. She's very active in social media platforms and her poems have also been published in various e-journals and translated into different languages.

The Book of Garcia Marquez
short story by Sherzod Artikov

I love October. There is more wind and rain in October. The weather is often cloudy. Yellow leaves rustle under your feet, and a leaffall brings peace and comfort to your heart.

Yesterday it was windy, but today it rained. By evening, though it was quiet, the bitterness that came from the ground, and its wet smell was still lingering in my breath. In the evening, the temperature dropped very low, so I cooled down on the balcony. Then I went inside.

In my cozy room there was a long and large bookshelf. I went up to it and for a moment thought about what to do. I was not inclined to read. My head hurt and my heart was beating. It is unlikely that a book would help in such a situation.

When I fell down on a chair, I remembered again that Nafisa had not come for the book. She took Marquez's "One hundred years of solitude" exactly ten days ago. Since then, she has not been seen.

As time passed, the headache increased. I took a medicine and drank a freshly brewed bitter coffee in addition. After that, I started walking back and forth in the room.

...In the house across the street from me lived a Russian old woman. She died two months ago, and Nafisa and her family moved into her apartment. The old woman's son, who lived abroad, sold the house to them. Nafisa's father was military, worked in the military part of the city, and she herself, if I am not mistaken, taught English at school.

She must have heard from her neighbors that I have a private library. She herself never asked about it. When she met me in the street, she just nodded to greet me, without saying anything, it was probably inconvenient to ask for something.

"Can I read something from your books?" she asked me once, suddenly appearing in front of my apartment.

At first, I was very surprised. Nobody here asked me for books. Nevertheless, I invited her inside.

"You have so many books!"

She looked around my library and rejoiced like a little child. I stood silently in front of the window, pressing a cigarette to my lips. I did not want to answer her. I thought that then she would ask more questions. I was used to not answering anybody when I was smoking.

"Can I take Jack London's book?" she asked.

I nodded as a sign of consent, inhaling cigarette smoke and turning my back on her. Nafisa took the book and thanked me from the bottom of her heart.

"Thank you very much! I will read it quickly!"

Her first book was "Martin Eden". Then she began to come to me in every three or four days. We almost did not communicate, she was a little confused, especially when she saw that I do not pay attention to her. When she noticed how indifferent I was smoking at the window, she would carefully return the book she had read to the shelf and hurriedly leave.

Eventually, it turned into our routine. But for the last time, everything was different. I don't even know why. This time, I did not smoke at the window. On the contrary, I sat in a chair and did not take my eyes off her. She was in no hurry to leave, too, leaving a book. She stood in front of the shelf longer than usual, as if she could not choose. After a long pause, she took Marquez's "One hundred years of solitude" and looked at it with interest, standing in the center of the room.

"It turns out that you like to read world literature?" I asked for the first time, looking at her closely.

When she caught my look, she blushed like a beet.

"Yes, I often read world literature," she said, maintaining her composure and continued to flip through the pages of the book.

Perhaps, she was not attractive. Nevertheless, her polite behavior, smooth movements, calm confidence and at the same time the thirst for life, shining in her eyes, were extremely attractive.

"Have you read all these books?"

"Almost," I said after looking at the closet.

"I envy you," she continued, closing the book and going to leave.

"Would you like to have a cup of coffee?" I asked, suddenly standing up when she reached the doorstep. "Today is the right weather for coffee."

Nafisa looked out the open window.

"Well, if it doesn't give you any trouble..." she said confusedly.

"Do you want sugar or no sugar?"

"Let it be without sugar."

For coffee, I forgot my inhumanity and shyness. I spoke with enthusiasm about the books I read and my favorite authors. She listened to me with interest and attention. When it was her turn, she spoke with pleasure and no less enthusiasm. Listening to her, I realized that I was fascinated by a man whose worldview was like mine, like two drops of water, and that I finally felt the sweet pleasure that had been lacking in my life for many years.

When she left, I was again alone with my books. As it always was. I was very much mistaken, expecting that my heart, accustomed to loneliness, would again begin to wander quietly in its deserted corners. For the first time, I felt deeply alone, feeling the fullness of this dark feeling in four walls.

When I left the house the next day, I accidentally met Nafisa in the street. Her sister was with her on her way to school. As always, I greeted her, but we walked silently to the bus stop. I wanted to talk, but then I thought about it. Maybe I was embarrassed again because of the people around me.

At the bus stop, I caught a cab and she got on the bus. On the way I remembered the book she had taken the last time.Then I began to wonder if she would read it quickly. In the end, I decided firmly that she would succeed.

Four days passed without any news. On the fifth absence Nafisa squeezed the peace of mind out of my soul. On the sixth, contrary to my nature, my heart fell, and I began to get very nervous. On the seventh day, as usual smoking at the window, I came to the conclusion that it is impossible to finish reading this book by Marquez for a week, and this conclusion led me to seizures.

Yesterday my state of mind deteriorated and I could not concentrate on my work in the insurance company. I had no idea how I could read a 386-page book for so long, and I constantly thought about it. Other obsessive thoughts were dreaming in my head. Probably, Nafisa had no time to read the book, I said to myself. After a minute I thought she just did not like the book and forgot to return it.

Most of my colleagues were not interested in reading it, except for Feruza Anvarovna from the Risk Management Department. She was about thirty five years old - she was a sincere and very smart woman. During the break, I wanted to ask her about this book by Marquez, which occupied all my mind.

"Feruza Anvarovna," I said while entering. "Can I ask you something?"

At that time she was sorting stacks of papers on her desk.

"Of course, Humayun."

"How many days will you read a book with three hundred and eighty-six pages?"

Feruza Anvarovna thought a little.

"It depends on what kind of book it is. If I am interested in it, I will finish reading it in seven days. If not, I will not read it even in a month."

A little bit later I addressed to one of my clients with the same question.

"If I try, probably, to read it within two weeks," he said after thinking.

On the way home, the cab driver also asked the same question.

"Honestly, I'm not interested in reading books," he said, sneaking around through my rearview mirror.

When I got home, I stood in the hallway, leaning against the wall without going inside. This had an ulterior purpose: if Nafisa had seen me from her window, she would probably have come to change the book. I stood like this for twenty minutes. But there was no knocking on the door. When I was disappointed, I put my hand in my pants pocket and took out a pack of cigarettes. The box was almost empty.

Fortunately, there was the last cigarette left. It helped me to distract a little: I went to the bookshelf and took some books from there. One had two hundred and fifty-four pages, the other one had one hundred and eighty three, and the third one had one hundred and twenty-four pages. I left this third one and put the rest back on the shelf. Having flipped through the book from beginning to end, I decided to recommend it to Nafisa next time...

...Wandering around the room soon tired my legs. I leaned on the back of the chair. The pain in my head began to fade after taking a pill. But my heart was still pounding like crazy. Having put my head on the edge of the chair, I closed my eyes for a moment. The image of Nafisa swam before my eyes again and again. Then I realized that the discomfort, nervousness, bad mood for the last ten days were all the result of waiting. I, accustomed since childhood not to expect anything, was looking forward to meeting her as nothing else. I was looking forward to seeing her again, how she would talk to me and her pleasant voice would fill the room. Why should I lie to myself? After all, it really did not matter how long the book by Marquez was read.

When I admitted this fact, I suddenly laughed. My laughter was full of pain, longing and sadness. I kept laughing. My voice was getting louder and louder. At that moment, there was a knock on the door. At first, I did not pay attention. Then somebody knocked again. Before opening, I corrected my tie and buttoned my shirt. After that, I opened it. Nafisa was standing on the threshold holding a book in her hand.

"I hardly finished," she said, trying to smile and showing me the book in her hand. "Marquez made me sweat a lot."

Translated into English by the author

Sherzod Artikov was born in 1985 in the city of Marghilan of Uzbekistan. He graduated from Fergana Polytechnic institute in 2005. He was one of the winners of the national literary contest " My Pearl Region " in the direction of prose in 2019. In 2020, his first authorship book " The Autumn's Symphony " was published in Uzbekistan by publishing house "Yangi Asr Avlodi" . In 2021, his works were published in the anthology books called " World Writers " in Bangladesh, "Asia sings" and " Mediterranean Waves " in Egypt, "Emerging horizons" in India, " Healing through verses" in Canada in English language and his authorship book " The autumn's symphony" was published in Spanish and English in Cuba by Argos Iberoamericana Publishing House.

ADVERTISEMENT

May Queen   - Lynn White

They crowned her the queen of May,

the little girl.

Chose her for her purity.

Pure and white and smiling.

Unblooded.

Golden curls

held by red ribbons,

and entwined with flowers

topped with sweet smelling may.

Spring is here,

you see.

New shoots springing into life,

so we're ready to be

reborn and ready to play

the game.

Ready for the circle.

Ready to go

round and round again.

Like the dancers she watches

weaving their ribbons round

the maypole.

The maypole phallus they've planted

in the ground and

bedecked with ribbons.

Red and white.

Red and white ribbons of menstrual blood

and semen.

Round and round

She watches from her throne.

Round and round.

Then come the Morris Men.

Bells jangling their presence.

Sticks clashing with their power.

Flags waving

to announce

their virility.

They crowned her the queen of May,

the little girl.

A crown of sweet blossom

and hidden thorns.

First Published by Community Arts Ink, Reclaiming Our Voices, 2015

Lynn White lives in north Wales. Her work is influenced by issues of social justice and events, places and people she has known or imagined. She was shortlisted in the Theatre Cloud 'War Poetry for Today' competition and has been nominated for a Pushcart Prize, Best of the Net and a Rhysling Award.

Find Lynn at:

https://lynnwhitepoetry.blogspot.com and
https://www.facebook.com/Lynn-White-Poetry-1603675983213077/

WOMEN AND FICTION
Q & A with W. Ruth Kozak

Thank you for joining World Inkers Monthly Magazine for a discussion on women and fiction. Would you say there is a difference in the ways male writers and female writers characterize women in their stories? What differences would you note?

In some stories there may be. It depends if the story is male focused. I don't read romances but in those the women are often portrayed as 'weaker' than the men.

Complex characters drive a narrative. How do you develop a complex character? What sort of conflicts would a woman protagonist face in contrast to a male?

I write historicals and in those the women face a lot of challenges that modern women don't. I think the female characters in these stories need to have some strong goal in mind and be willing to fight for their rights in spite of the male dominance.

Is there a dearth of female representations in fiction? And of those you are familiar with, are they positive representations? Do you think male characterizations have more or less depth in contemporary fiction than female characters?

I enjoy historicals with women protagonists. Margaret George's "Memoirs of Cleopatra'" Paulline Gedge" "the Eagle and the Raven"; Manda Scott" Boudica"; Marion Zimmer Bradley "The Mists of Avalon" Mary Renault "Fire From Heaven" in which she introduces Alexander's very tough mother, Olympias. All these novels, set in Egypt and ancient Britain have very strong female protagonists.

Are there differences between men and women literature can address?

Just give the women an equal 'voice' to the men. Show their strength, especially in dire times.

How can literature shape the cultural ground we stand on for support? Can stronger and more thoughtful female representations lead to a better understanding of female empowerment and the need for it in the literary field?

I definitely think so. Women need to read these kinds of historicals to get a sense of what kind of life women lived long ago – not pampered and indulged but having to work hard and even go to battle for their rights.

Who is a leading female character you admire?

Boudica is a very strong character in British history (the time of when the Romans entered Britain). I've always been fascinated by her. And more recently, the Diary of Anne Frank, knowing what that young girl went through during WWII. And of course, Olympias, Alexander the Great's mother . My next novel will be about her. My current W.I.P. DRAGONS IN THE SKY is in the first person narrative of a young Cymru (Welsh) girl who is kidnapped by a renegade warriors chief's son and taken across Europe, eventually rescued by Alexander as a youthful hunter. He turns her over to a Greek physician where she learns the skills of a healer and eventually, after a grueling trek, returns to her people.

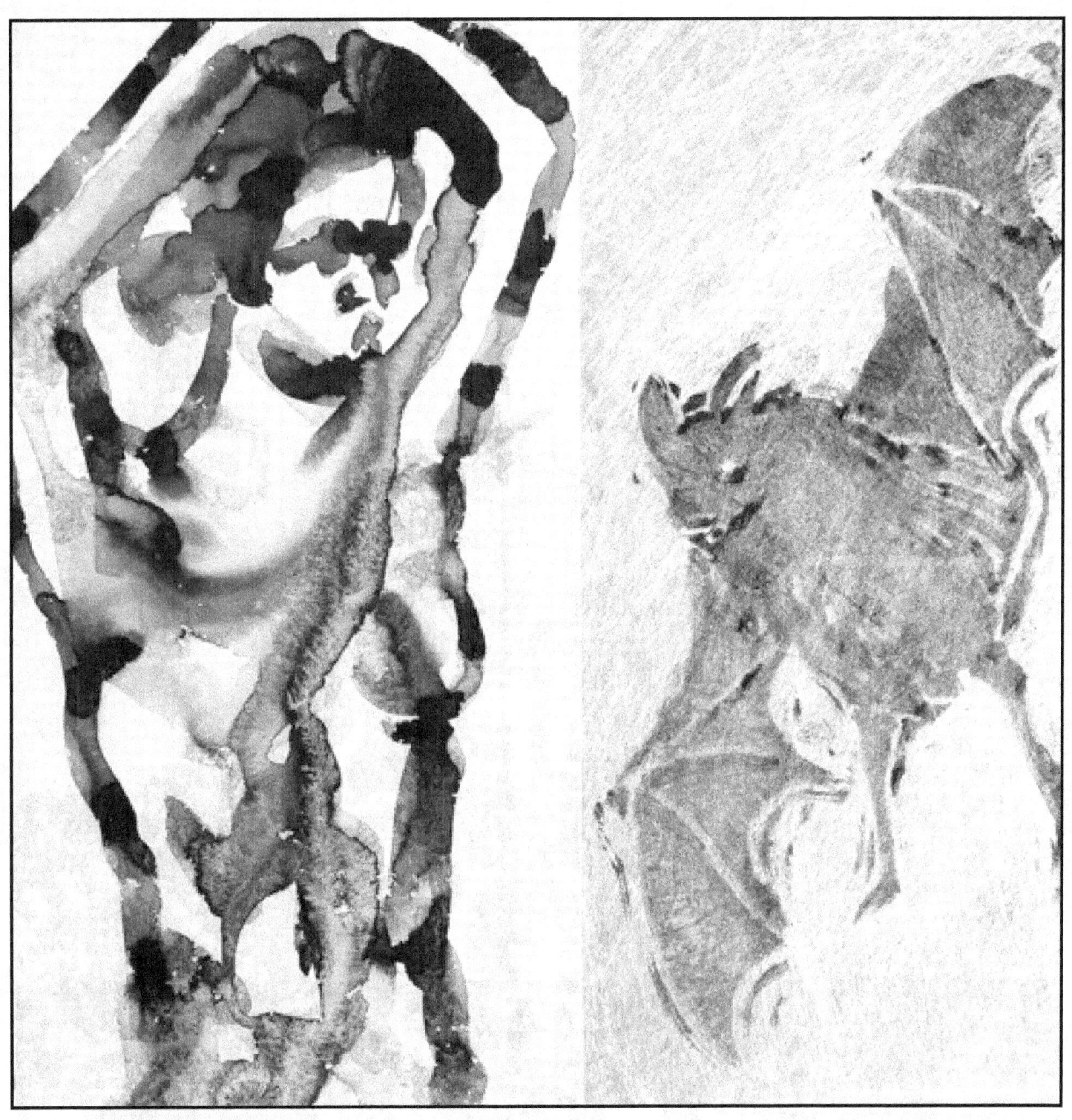

Woman with Bat by Cynthia Yachtman

Woman Means Power

- Bogdana Găgeanu

Not only men, but women had power, too
Think about Lady Macbeth or Cleopatra
Think about the Amazons
Beautiful women, ready to fight.
The empire of women is very old
Women were independent since old times.
Nowadays, think about 'The iron lady'!
We have engineer women, pilot women
Even president women.
They are not only mothers and wives.
Women are smart
Being smart is beautiful
Men were always attracted by intelligent women
And they wanted to conquer them.
Women are flowers who have the strength of a tree
Souls protected by a powerful shield!

Profundity photo by Carl Scharwath

Japanese Women of the Sun

- Maki Starfied

In the beginning, Japanese women were the sun.
They were true human beings.
They did not want to be the moon.
But today's Japanese women are sickly, pale-faced moons who live by Japanese men and shine by their light.
If I reproach them, "You are the ones who let this happen after all."
They lament, "We've suffered enough" or "Let bygones be bygones. We're not going to change anyway."

But it is you who did nothing; you are just the same people as you were before.
You still think that women are the moon, you fools!
Once you realize this, you will see your station, your status, and even your foolishness.
And your God will come.
Indeed, Japanese women are the sun.
There is true freedom.

The Forgotten Heroines

Essay by Dr. Venkat Kumaresan

Every positive change starts with inspiration. Women have contributed to many changes in society that have brought about a radical difference in the quality of life. The contributions of these women may have been lauded and celebrated then but at times history falters in its responsibility to pass on their achievements to posterity. The world, ignorant at large of past experiences, has been investing a lot of time in solving similar problems resulting in the loss of lives, opportunities, and money. These women in history had been successful in creating a huge impact on society when social media was unheard of. In today's world of astronomical communication progress, reflecting upon the acts of such women warriors can become a ready reckoner for countries facing troubled times.

Clint Eastwood once said, "Sometimes if you want to see a change for the better, you have to take things into your own hands."

"Vaccination" is today a byword for, a panacea for safety and well-being. Even as the world has faced a few pandemics before, the mass vaccination was not easy with that experience. It wasn't easy to gain acceptance. It had 'teething' challenges in the administration that could not be 'brushed' aside. If this is the case when telecommunications and healthcare have the best reach, can you imagine the situation had an epidemic broken in 1767? Smallpox was not a small problem then. It was handled systematically, carefully, and with a vision that countries can emulate from even now. Have you heard of Empress Maria Theresa? She was the Queen of Hungary and Austria. She was an admirable administrator who inspired popular leaders then. The emperor Napoleon had a statue of Maria Theresa in his office. She served as his inspiration. If leaders and bureaucrats of the present knew how Maria Theresa had resolved the smallpox pandemic then, the price we paid and are still paying to fight the present pandemic would have reduced greatly. What did Maria do differently, ahead of her time? She cared for every citizen. She realized that asking for support was not a sign of weakness. The Empress got Gerard van Swieten, a Dutch physician, to her kingdom. She sought help from Maria Antonia, the German princess. She tried inviting specialists from England. When that did not get through, she learned the current practices of smallpox inoculation in England. Thus, she tapped the collective intellect of countries to handle the crisis. Maria Theresa's intelligence in tapping international resources successfully, while maintaining a cordial relationship with the nations, would be a lesson that would greatly benefit the world if leaders today followed her ways. It would definitely help save precious human lives.

It is important to bring the spread under control. Maria Theresa identified every practice that aggravated the situation. She realized the importance of social distancing. The Empress understood the unhygienic practices associated with burial. Hence, she ordered that no new burial grounds can come up without the consent of her government. This decelerated the spread of the disease.

Maria Theresa promoted inoculation in every possible way. Clinical trials were important. Even though the Royal physician was against her idea, she convinced him and started the trial. Since children were most vulnerable, she tried the vaccination on thirty-four newborn orphans and sixty-seven orphans aged between five and fourteen years. She did not consider their lives to be any less valuable. She got vaccinated and got her two children vaccinated too. That led people to believe in the vaccine.

She lived by the quote from the popular leadership life-guide book 'Father Of Your Team' – 'Leadership is not RACing ahead of others. Leadership is CARing ahead of others'. She wanted to encourage those who participated in the clinical trials. So, she hosted a dinner at the <u>Schönbrunn Palace</u> for those children who underwent clinical trials. Nations can derive inspiration in showing gratitude to the change agents by adopting her example.

Healthcare funds remained a challenge for most countries during each Covid wave. While kings and queens amass wealth from the public, the Empress contributed 22 million guldens (Dutch currency) her son had inherited, to the country's treasury. History may not repeat, Yet, the history of those practical and visionary leaders is relevant.

If that Empress could not be unseated from her throne, it was not easy to unseat an ordinary woman from her bus seat. Both were able to create a following. While the Empress combated a disease that needed social distancing, this woman made a surgical strike on Racial distancing. Her popularity was eclipsed by a leader inspired by her.

Rosa Louise McCauley Parks is her name. She was determined to prove that all individuals are equal. Racial discrimination was at its peak in Alabama. Colored and whites had different schools, places of worship, different lifts, and separate water fountains. On December 1, 1955, she took a stand on the rules of the bus. She was very tired that day after a long day at work. The rules required her to stand and give away her seat to the whites when they stepped in. She refused. The driver asked her to get down. She refused. The police took her to custody finally. Whether it was inside the bus or the police station, she remained unmoved.

She was asked to pay a fine of $10. Her color was not fair. That rule was not fair either. She appealed to the court for the law to be repealed. That night the African-Americans made a decision. They decided to boycott all the buses. Even if they are to travel long distances, they decided not to use a bus. It succeeded after being boycotted by the colored for 381 days! One of those who supported that movement and took inspiration from her was Martin Luther King Jr. 'Black Lives Matter' campaign changed the fortunes of politicians in the United States last year.

Most around the world may remember Martin Luther King Jr as the crusader of the Civil Rights movement. Yet the woman who cleaned up the houses of white people after school and also cleaned up the judicial system is not equally remembered.

Women have paved the way for dramatic cultural changes and have handled the world's biggest problems that are relevant even in today 's world. Reimagining current challenges from the perspective of those Women leaders and reflecting upon them will help us make constructive decisions and make the world a beautiful place to live.

I acknowledge the contribution of my school English teacher Ms. Meena Suresh toward reviewing this essay.

Dr. Venkat Kumaresan is the award-winning author of Amazon US #1 New Release- 'Father of Your Team', Workplace Challenges Guru, humorist, keynote speaker, storyteller, blogger, coach, and poet. Venkat has written over 50 poems with some of them featuring in popular anthologies like 'Over the Rainbow' children anthology, 'My Mother' anthology for World Book of Records, UK, and he has presented poems in the International Spring Festival, Paper Fiber Fest, etc. Venkat promotes young super-achievers through an entertaining program titled 'Arattai with Achievers` through the Youtube Channel : Author Venkat. Through a cartoon-based session, Author Venkat had trained girl children of domestic help and maintenance workers on leadership.

Rosa Parks from public domain

Olga Levadnaya

woman

Mustafa Gökçek

Over the crown of the apple tree of sadness
a rainbow appeared
after the rain.
The flabby bark of the tree
gathered in its wrinkles.
The twigs streamed
to meet the midday
sun,
and a ringing necklace of birds
shuddered
at every blowing of the wind.
Their polyphony
would be heard
from over the horizon
of my desires.
Smoke
drifted
from the neighbouring garden.

Adam and Eve
flooded the bath house.

Trans. Richard McCain

When I look at you suddenly
My eyes are fading to the horizon
How emotional are your green eyes
The love that smells in those eyes

My suffering, my life is in you
You are life, you are hope, you are my remedy
Your eyes are different, your lips are different
I am saddened by your moistened heart

When I can't hug happily
I found you, with my heart on the horizon
And you're my woman, my woman, my bread
I have a nice eye tonight

Who came, who passed
you have been the candle of my life
I loved you, woman, my way has been enlightened
However, no one has ever been loved as much as you.

My longing, you colored my life
My feelings were exhilarated for months
The birds of distant lands sing at the snowy window
Life takes the heart to that window

Olga Levadnaya is a Russian poet renowned in the world, she was awarded titles of the Honored Worker of Culture of the Republic of Tatarstan in 2008 and laureate of the State prize named after Gavriil Derzhavin in 2007, State prize named after Sajida Suleymanova in 2015. She was nominated for the "International Peace Award". Olga is a member of the Writers Union of the Republic of Tatarstan, Writers Union of the Russian Federation and International Writers Union. She is the Art Director of the Kazan poetic theatre "Dialogue".Olga Levadnaya has written books: "My Life is Waiting for Snow" (1992), "Passing the Enchanted Circle "(1998), "Falling up Free" (2003), "Close to our Past" (2003), "Climbing the Ladder of Thoughts" (2005), "From the Cry of Birds Memories Grow" (2005), "Star gate" (2010), "Wind of the Heart " (2014), favorites in two volumes (2022). In 2020, book "Vocal works on poems by Olga Levadnaya" was published. O.Levadnaya is the organizer of the Russian music and poetry festivals "Handshake of the Republics" (2017-2021).

Mustafa Gökçek was born on 02.10.1953 in Gaziantep. He completed his primary school in the city where he was born, secondary and high school education, settled in İzmir and continued his studies and life here. Writer / Poet / Playwright and theater instructor-director Mustafa Gökçek, after these studies, completed his High School education in Ankara, DTCF. Author, TYS (Turkish Writers' Union), PEN (International Writers' Union), TÜRKGEB (Founder of Turkish Young Writers' Union), İZMES (Founder-President of İzmir Literature-Art Group) TÜRKYES (Turkey Publishing, Literature, Art - Founder, Honorary President) is a member of İZSES (Founder of İzmir Art and Literature Conversations) and the International Union of Activist Artists, and currently continues to write in the newspaper "Haber Hürriyet" and the website-newspaper www.haberhürriyet.com-.

Maki Starfield, a poet, a translator and a painter, born in Ehime, 1972. She earned her Master of Arts from Sophia University, getting the diploma of International business management and the certificate of TESOL in Canada. She is a representative in Japan of Immagine Poesia, a member of Japan Universal Poets Association, and Japanese haiku associates. She has been honored with the following: Guido Gozzano Prize (Honorable Mention) 2018,2019; Naji Naaman Literary Prize (Creativity) 2020; Pushcart prize nomination 2020; and, Sahitto International Award for Literature 2021.

Prayer of Revered Lips by Gourab Chakraborty

Poetry in translation by Jagari Mukherjee

1
Prayer of revered lips--
the script is black and white.
The words are Divine-black
and the pages are Devotee-light.
The lovemaking of sorrow and pain
and that of the alphabet
of heard visions and visual phonemes
I have knitted once and again.

Yet seem uncontrolled, the names of each sound dripping.
Next to a poem, Creation and Concoction are sleeping.

2
Am I an outsider? Am I so helpless?
They abandon me from Memory's inner recess.
Not light but darkness--my past-traveling voice
renders be bleeding in each alphabetical choice.

Every time I bleed, I am reincarnated.
I devour the unheard, unspoken, unwritten phonemes
till I am sated.

3
Twilight knows prohibition, Life knows its end;
under the final line my time quietly I'd spend.
The stillness indeed, under the symbol of Time
desires profound meaning, to live, to die,
under the requirement of rhyme.

The Poet thinks, it is a profoundly distant relationship:
aloud he says--make me bleed more deep.

4
Before witnesses I say, every day I surrender.
Beside dead light, fireflies lone tears render.
Not tears! A salt birth! in the hidden embryo of pain.
Every feather knows, that shedding is in Fate's inevitable lane.

In the Horizon's touch, a moment is treasured.
The Poet dies in every phoneme as Life is measured.

5
The lights are illuminated one by one
And once again they fade and are gone.
One by one the years roll away.
Little by little in poems I turn astray.
Yet it is Poetry that keeps me alive.

I have no demands, no questions nor any say.
Life--today we have strife,
tomorrow we'll be friends anyway.

Translated from Bengali

Gourab Chakraborty

Jagari Mukherjee

The Female Vortex in Blues Music

interview with Angie Mack, creative musical consultant

Angie, we introduced you in the first edition of *World Inkers Monthly Magazine*. I hope you were impressed with your name on the cover! What would you say specifically about the Blues and your relationship to this style of music? Can you tell us about its development as an art form?

Thank you so much for highlighting me in your first edition of World Inkers Monthly Magazine and for the great work that you do in promoting writers!

The interesting quality about the blues is that it began as a uniquely American artform. However, its presence in American music curriculum is grossly underrepresented. Music curriculum still places a heavy emphasis on European classical musicians. The blues does not get the credence that I believe it should in American classrooms. I was a Music Theory Major at a Wisconsin state university for a time. It was disappointing to be taught that blues and rock were somehow inferior genres because of their emphasis on the I - IV - V chords. However, the brilliance in the blues is not in the technicality but in the invocation of feeling. It is expressionistic. Blues was created as an emotional release to oppression. It was created as a means of human expression and authentic communication. It was used as an alternate form of making a living. Somehow, music educators have believed the lie that emotional music is somehow inferior. I beg to differ.

Musically speaking, what characterizes the Blues from other traditional forms such as folk or gospel?

The roots of both folk and gospel music are rooted in the blues. I recently watched a CBS YouTube video of Mick Jagger and Keith Richards of the Rolling Stones explaining how blues musicians such as Big Bill Broonzy, Brownie McGhee and Sonny Terry fueled the American folk music revival. Musicians in America and abroad began listening to and learning how to play like the early acoustic blues players. Early blues songs were remade and recorded in the 1960s such as "I'm So Glad" original to Skip James but made popular by the band Cream.

The Father of Gospel music is Thomas A. Dorsey who was also a key musical director and arranger for the Paramount record label based out of southeastern Wisconsin. Thomas A. Dorsey was one of the first to be inducted into the Paramount Plaza Walk of Fame in Grafton, WI. His most popular gospel song, "Precious Lord" continues to move audiences to this day. It was a favorite of Dr. Martin Luther King as well as performed by Mahalia Jackson and Aretha Franklin. Thomas A. Dorsey's influence on American music and R&B is grossly underrepresented.

Were women treated as significant in Blues culture? Since the culture emerged from oppression of Blacks, did that affect the ability to see women recognized as integral to the music itself?

Women paved the way for the popularization of blues music. Mamie Smith's "Crazy Blues" recording pioneered the way for other female blues giants. The popularity of that one recording convinced talent scouts to find more. As a result, Paramount blues recording artists such as Gertrude "Ma" Rainey, Ethel Waters and Alberta Hunter found their songs playing on "victrolas" in homes across the nation.

Who are some prominent Blues women? How did their legacies impact the musical landscape?

Paramount blues artist Hattie McDaniel recorded "Dentist Chair Blues". She also was the first black American to receive an Oscar for her role in "Gone with the Wind". Ethel Waters was the first black woman to star in her own radio show on NBC. Gertrude "Ma" Rainey was a diva who also inspired literary works such as August Wilson's "Ma Rainey's Black Bottom". Trixie Smith needs to be given more credit for coining the term "Rock and Roll" in her song, "My Daddy Rocks Me". Alberta Hunter is considered one of the first to perform American blues music in Europe.

What advice would you offer to today's gifted female musicians? Is the landscape improving for them? What might young artists expect?

Advice for today's female musicians? As someone with a multi-decade career in music, I advise other women to demand respect and reciprocation. Women are NOT treated equally especially as it relates to pay and opportunities of leadership and production. Speak out against objectification and age as being a precursor for financial success.

What route to cultural inclusivity for female musicians do you suggest? Did the Blues music and culture open doors for female participation in the arts?

It is statistically true that most music and music events are produced by men. I am a female producer by nature and still scratching my head on how I can make a living as a producer. I have self produced a few albums and started a hobby record label called Hot Seat Records. I started a Patreon account with the hopes of donations to work on producing a musical. I am heavily qualified to produce a musical. However, I seem perpetually stuck in the field of teaching because it's the only way to pay the bills. Lack of funding and leadership opportunities are grossly missing. Covid has made the music industry for women even worse. Professional momentum gained prior to Covid has been lost making the industry excruciatingly tough and competitive. WE NEED MORE FEMALE CREATORS.

Finally, when you are at home what are your favorite Blues artists who inspire you to be more active in creating music?

I get in ruts. Listening repetitively to music in the background is how I learn. These days, I am stuck on Boogie Woogie pianist Meade Lux Lewis. He was actually in the Nick's Bar scene of It's a Wonderful Life but was not recognized in the credits. When he was just 22 years old, he recorded "Honky Tonk Train Blues" for Paramount Records which is considered foundational in Rock and Roll. The energy in his music is insane! It inspires me as I consider myself a rhythm pianist. Yes, I have been known to pound so hard on pianos as to break them! Unleashed frustration much?

A familiar standard of mine is to listen to the pulsating guitar and smooth vocals of Mississippi John Hurt. My body literally becomes more relaxed. Because of this, I consider the music to be healing. I had the opportunity of interviewing one of his relatives named Fred Bolden. Fred is also the nephew of Skip James and is quite popular on the Internet.

The Importance of Women Writers...
Interview with *Jill Sharon Kimmelman*

Greetings Jill, and congratulations on being nominated a 2022 Woman of the Year by *World Inkers Monthly Magazine*! This issue is dedicated to women and changing the narratives about female empowerment. What does it mean to you to be a woman in the contemporary world?

First let me take a moment to thank you very much, for the extraordinary honor of including my name on a list of Woman Of The Year 2022 by *World Inkers Monthly Magazine* nominees.

I am most grateful to you & Mutiu for embracing, not only my work, you have both taken me into your hearts, a reason for celebration each & every day.

As I interact daily with poets & writers, I am awed & saddened to meet truly gifted women, who have no "safe brave space" or support from their family members or friends!

This culture of inequality exists throughout the world, in nations where poetry by men are called **"SIGNIFICANT ACHIEVEMENTS, HISTORIC BOOKS CONTRIBUTIONS TO WORLD LITERATURE"**

Women's milestones & their debuts are generally ignored.

So, how do we initiate an enormous, long-awaited, desperately-needed change for women everywhere?

How do we help women to become empowered, given a collective & individual voice that is recognized, not just to receive an equality, but to play a role in creating a new powerful presence in the world?

This place where women lead with powerful ideas, unburden their scarred hearts, & be recognized as a beautiful, inside & out, as a woman capable, competent, wise & compelling.

One is not born an "empowered woman". It is a title learned & earned, first in stories & updated fairytales. We sing songs & tell stories while a newborn sucks at our breast, or from a bottle, as we cradle them in our arms.

Be it a girl or a boy, it is essential that nurturing is completely equal. As young children begin to absorb comprehension skills, it is vital that they play together. Toddlers must be exposed to children of other races, skin colors & all genders.

Without those first five years of spoon-fed gentle rewarding examples, it is far more challenging to teach any child, boys & girls, the critical lessons of equality for ALL.

To engage in conversation with my brother & sister poets & writers, from every corner of our Mother Earth, it does not take long to see existing patterns. These are defined by a culture that freely dismisses women.

In the words of a dear friend, who taught herself to read, is an activist for women's rights, seeking to have laws change to allow all women, regardless of their birthright & living in a country where women are tortured, enslaved & deprived of the most rudimentary education, she shared this message.

"In my country there is little opportunity for women to have time for themselves. I received an education up to university level only because my father is a well-known highly-respected professor. For other women, they toil from sun up to sundown like a buffalo pulling a wagon. They have little food to nourish their exhausted bodies" & no access to proper medical care for their starving babes.

The way to break this sanctioned thousand year old culture is through the education of children, girls as well as boys. These children, nourished & valued, recognized as equals, inside their home, will carry those ingrained values to their school mates & throughout the adventure of play dates.

As a woman in 2022, living in the USA, it is remarkable that our citizens finally voted for an election ticket that had Vice President, Kamala Harris, an undeniable well-educated, former attorney general of California, & an empowered woman of color.

Congratulations to our Vice President. Is there anyone out there who is astonished that this historic milestone took over 200 years???

I applaud our President Joe Biden for promising & keeping that promise of bringing the best running mate to serve our country & to celebrate her commitment & dedication to shatter that final glass ceiling.

I rejoice at the public dismissal & zero tolerance policies that have occurred over the past 10-15 years, for women of every age & from every walk of life.

The "Me Too Movement" was born out of decades of the whispered outrage that tortured women whose names are instantly recognized. When these previously silent women came together to share their individual experiences, a whisper of singular voices became a collective chorus of protests, sparked by a culture that had always allowed & ignored harm, disrespect & inequality.

Those courageous women became a voice for the world to respect, admire, & of greatest importance, to model their own children, siblings, friends & the politicians that they elected to represent all of our citizens.

That is where poets, such as myself come in. We read & hear all of this happening in our country & on foreign shores. We rise in protest...our pens bleed with an empowered yearning & our voices finally are no longer dismissed.

Our words, carefully chosen, crafted into anthems, sage wisdom that begins when a child is born, knowledge, awareness & a promise of a healthy safe world for all is delivered with breast milk & shared between girls & boys sharing classrooms.

Considering the criticism by some contemporary Westernized feminists of men and types of masculinity, what can you say about human relationships in the coming era? When you hear the phrase 'toxic masculinity', what comes to mind?

When I read the phrase or engage in a conversation where the other person manifests evident "toxic masculinity", my first reaction is to run from that egocentric narcissist man attempting to draw me into conversations.

I choose not to run. I stay, primarily because this is an opportunity to demonstrate to him an empowered woman who is a SURVIVOR. After indulging him in a one-sided boastful conversation, I make my move. I take advantage of a pregnant pause & ask a question.

The question does not matter. All that matters is that my question has nothing to do with him or his likes & dislikes.

Immediately he is flustered. I see it in his eyes, where emotions we try to hide, always betray us. This big man with hubris & ignorance goes down the rabbit hole. Queen wins: Checkmate!

That's what happens when I hear that new normal phrase!

What are some strengths of being a woman? What would you tell men about being a woman in today's world landscape?

To be a woman in 2022 in my country, USA, actively pursuing a career as a respected successful poet is not difficult, but only if **SUCCESSFUL** is defined as having nothing to do with financially lucrative!

I have yet to encounter any poets ,in my own country, who are able to support, or even supplement, their full time careers.

We write because we don't know how not to. When to not write will be the certain death of our spirit.

Poetry in the USA is enjoying a surprise awareness, thanks in part to the historic event, seen round the world at the inauguration of President Joe Biden, in January of 2021: that magical memorable moment when a young woman of color, by the name of Amanda Gorman, in a bright yellow coat stood on the steps of the inaugural stage & stunned the world with a magnificent performance of her poem. It expressed a history of shame & offered an unparalleled, unprecedented & unforgettable vision for an equality that embraces EVERYONE.

Her poem spoke to people, men, women & children not only cheered, clapped & pumped fists for the promise of HOPE.

Poets everywhere found their long-shuttered youthful passion & began to write again. During the global pandemic, books of poetry spilled forth from women, men & children as young as 7 years old.

No longer are voices silent. Righteous anger, protest against policies & cultures of dismissive, disrespectful, & discrimination are slowly dissolving into history.

That is still not a reality in much of our world, with unacceptable behavior in places where women still remain enslaved, raped, displaced, struggling, against ancient laws of bias & religious beliefs.

Even in these countries, woman poets have created a new order, proclaimed their rights & marched for change.

How can men advocate best for women in a culture such as ours today?

We will stand as one. We will educate the next generation & practice what we preach. As poets have done since the time of Plato & Socrates, we will not let our words go unsaid.

Poets, writers, artists, will you join with us to inspire our children's children with our God-given gifts & live long enough to witness freedom & equality for a woman, once denied & discarded, now strong, proud, empowered?

WORLD INKERS MONTHLY MAGAZINE

TOP TEN FEMALE LITERARY LUMINARIES 2022

LEZA CANTORAL

Leza Cantoral is the author of *Cartoons in the Suicide Forest* & *Trash Panda*. She's the Editor in Chief of CLASH Books & *Black Telephone Magazine*. She lives upstate New York with her family & her ghosts.

WORLD INKERS MONTHLY MAGAZINE

TOP TEN FEMALE LITERARY LUMINARIES 2022

KATE HANSON FOSTER

Kate Hanson Foster is the author of *Mid Drift*, a finalist for the Massachusetts Center for the Book Award. Her writing has appeared in *Birmingham Poetry Review, Comstock Review, Harpur Palate, Poet Lore, Salamander, Tupelo Quarterly*, and elsewhere. A recipient of the NEA Parent Fellowship through the Vermont Studio Center, she lives and writes in Groton, Massachusetts.

WORLD INKERS MONTHLY MAGAZINE

TOP TEN FEMALE LITERARY LUMINARIES 2022

EVA PETROPOULOU-LIANOU

Eva Petropoulou-Lianou was born in Xylokastro, Greece. Initially she loved journalism and in 1994 she worked as a journalist for the French newspaper "Le Libre Journal" but her love for Greece won her over and she returned in 2002. She has published books and eBooks: "Me and my other self, my shadow" Saita publications, "Geraldine and the Lake elf" in English - French, as well as "The Daughter of the Moon", in the 4th edition, in Greek - English, Oselotos publications. Her work has been included in the Greek Encyclopedia Haris Patsis, p. 300. Her books have been approved by the Ministry of Education and Culture of Cyprus, for the Student and Teacher library. Her new books, "The Fairy of the Amazon Myrtia "dedicated to Myrto with a disability, and" Lefkadios Hearn, Myths and Stories of the Far East ", illustrated by Sumi-e painter Dina Anastasiadou, are released in 2019. She recently published her book," The Adventures of Samurai Nogas san "in English by the publishing house OntimeBooks, based in England. Collaborates with the electronic literary magazine The poet magazine. She is his partner International Literary Union based in America. Collaborates for the promotion of literature and promotes the work of Greek poets. Eva is a member of the "Association Alia Mundi Serbia", the "International Society of Writers and Artists of Greece" and the "Piraeus Society of Letters and Arts" as well as the Corinthian Writers Society.

WORLD INKERS MONTHLY MAGAZINE

TOP TEN FEMALE LITERARY LUMINARIES 2022

SUFIA KHATOON

A multi-lingual performance poet, artist, literary translator and facilitator, **Sufia Khatoon** has authored two books of poetry – "Death in the Holy Month" (shortlisted for Yuva Puraskar by Sahitya Akademi, 2020), and "Ger-mi-na-tion" (The Red River Publication) and has won The Kavi Salam Award, 2018. Her works have appeared in various periodicals and anthologies like Indian Literature Journal, Bengaluru Review, Mad Swirl, Indian Periodical, Narrow Road Review, Poetry Dialogue, The Yearbook of Indian Poetry in English 20-21, Kolkata Cadence, Shape of a Poem, etc. Also forthcoming anthologies like North Indian Language anthology by Sahitya Akademi. She has presented her poems in major festivals like The Festival of Letters, Avishkar Young Writer's Festival, Dibrugarh, 2019 by Sahitya Academi, Apeejay Kolkata Literary Festival 2019-20, etc. After acclaim for her installation "300 Peace Poetry Prayer Flag", she has been inspired to collect poems from poets from world over and build installations throughout her life. As a Co-Founder of Rhythm Divine, she has curated various global events. She has an MA in English Literature, a PG in Journalism and Mass Communication and a Diploma in Visual Arts and Design.

WORLD INKERS MONTHLY MAGAZINE

TOP TEN FEMALE LITERARY LUMINARIES 2022

AMY FERRIS

Amy Ferris is an author, editor, screenwriter and playwright. Her screen adaptation of J. California Cooper's short story, **Funny Valentines** (Director: Julie Dash) was nominated for a Best Screenplay Award (BET, Black Reel). Her other screen credits include the feature: **Mr. Wonderful** (Director: Anthony Minghella), and the series, **Jack's Place** (Scott Brazil, Director, Showrunner - CBS). Amy curated two anthologies: **Dancing at The Shame Prom (co-editor),** and **Shades of Blue - Writers on Depression and Feeling Blue** (both published by Seal Press) and is a contributor to numerous anthologies. In 2012, **Marrying George Clooney** was adapted into an Off-Broadway play. I n 2018, Amy was honored with Women's eNews prestigious award **21 LEADERS FOR THE 21ST CENTURY.** In 2020, Amy co-authored **OLD SCHOOL LOVE** (HarperCollins Publishers) with Rev Run of Run DMC fame. S he was recently named one of NextTribe's **WOMEN of the Year 2021.** Amy is the Director of **Story Summit Writer's School.** She is on the Advisory board of **The Women's Media Center** and a co-founder of **Milford Readers and Writers Festival.** She is currently finishing her next memoir, **The Mess of Love** for SheWritesPress, Pub Date: 2023.

Funny Valentines

WORLD INKERS MONTHLY MAGAZINE

TOP TEN FEMALE LITERARY LUMINARIES 2022

KASHIANA SINGH

Kashiana Singh(http://www.kashianasingh.com/) calls herself a work practitioner and embodies the essence of her TEDx talk - Work as Worship into her everyday. Her chapbook Crushed Anthills from Yavanika Press in 2020 is a journey that unravels memory through 10 cities. She proudly serves as a Managing Editor for Poets Reading the News and her voice be read and heard on various international platforms. Kashiana's

first poetry collection is called, Shelling Peanuts and Stringing Words. Her newest full-length collection, Woman by the Door has just been released with Apprentice House Press. Kashiana lives in North Carolina and carries her various geopolitical homes within her poetry. Her poems have been published on various platforms. Besides being a learner of poetry, Kashiana's latest corporate assignment of 16 years was as Vice President, Health and Benefits Operations with Alight Solutions.

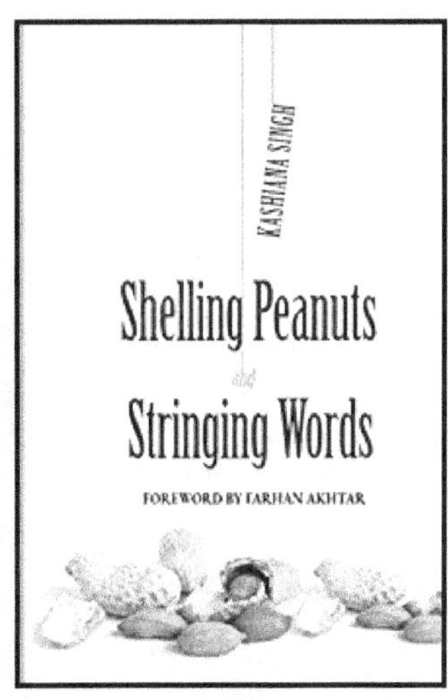

WORLD INKERS MONTHLY MAGAZINE

TOP TEN FEMALE LITERARY LUMINARIES 2022

STUTI SHREE

Stuti Shree is assistant editor for *Harbinger Asylum*, a literary journal that lasted 12 years on the poetry scene. In 2013, the journal was nominated by National Poetry Awards for best poetry magazine. Her service to the journal propelled its image magnificently to subscribers and its reading public. Stuti has a B.A. degree in English literature from St. Xavier's College in Ranchi, India.

WORLD INKERS MONTHLY MAGAZINE

TOP TEN FEMALE LITERARY LUMINARIES 2022

LEAH HUETE DE MAINES

Leah Huete de Maines (better known as Leah Maines) served as the senior editor for Finishing Line Press 2002-2017. Maines has edited hundreds of poetry collections, including several award-winning titles. She is Poet-in-Residence Emerita of Northern Kentucky University (funded in part by the Kentucky Humanities Council and the National Endowment for the Humanities). Maines is the author of two poetry books. Her

first book Looking to the East with Western Eyes, launched the New Women's Voices Series, No. 1 (Finishing Line Press, 1998), and reached #10 in the "Cincinnati/Tri-State Best Sellers List" (Cincinnati Enquirer), and is now in its fourth printing. Her most recent collection, Beyond the River, (KWC Press, 2002, 1st edition) won the Kentucky Writers' Coalition Poetry Chapbook Competition. Her poems have appeared in numerous national and international publications including Nebo, Owen Wister Review, Licking River Review, Flyway and other literary magazines and anthologies. Maines lived in Gifu, Japan where she studied and researched classical Japanese poetry at Gifu University. She studied English literature at Kings College London, England, and The Marino Institute in Dublin, Ireland. She studied publishing at Yale School of Management (SOM). Leah Huete de Maines (she/her) is mixed race LatinX / Creole / Sephardic Jewish.

WORLD INKERS MONTHLY MAGAZINE

TOP TEN FEMALE LITERARY LUMINARIES 2022

MARIA NAZOS

Poet, translator, and memoirist **Maria Nazos** has been published in *The New Yorker, TriQuarterly, World Literature Today, The Columbia Review, The Denver Quarterly, The Mid-American Review, American Life in Poetry, The Greensboro Review, The North American Review, The Tampa Review, Anomaly, The Florida Review, The Southern Humanities Review, The New Ohio Review, Tupelo Quarterly*, and elsewhere. A Pushcart nominee, her work has appeared in renowned anthologies including *What Saves Us: Poems of Empathy and Outrage in the Age of Trump*, (Northwestern University Press, 2020) edited by Martín Espada, and *Nasty Women, An Unapologetic Anthology of Subversive Verse*, edited by Grace Bauer and Julie Kane (Lost Horse Press, 2017). Maria is the author of two collections of poetry: *Still Life* (Dancing Girl Press 2016) and *A Hymn That Meanders* (Wising Up Press 2011). She served for three years as Ted Kooser's editorial assistant for his "American Life in Poetry" nationally-syndicated column. She holds an MFA in Writing from Sarah Lawrence College and PhD in English with a Creative Writing Emphasis and minor in Women's and Gender Studies from The University of Nebraska-Lincoln. Her work has received an Academy of American Poets Award, a Tennessee Williams Scholarship from The Sewanee Writers' Conference, scholarships from The Santa Fe Art Institute, The Provincetown Fine Arts Work Center, The Squaw Valley Community of Writers, and fellowships from The University of Nebraska, The Vermont Studio Center, The Kimmel Harding Nelson Center for the Arts, and The Virginia Center for the Creative Arts.

WORLD INKERS MONTHLY MAGAZINE

TOP TEN FEMALE LITERARY LUMINARIES 2022

JILL SHARON KIMMELMAN

Jill Sharon Kimmelman who is a Pushcart Prize nominee in poetry & has been nominated for the Best Of the Net 2018. Her critically acclaimed poems & recitations of other poets' work have garnered accolades, awards, & recognitions. By earning her place in the global poetry community, Jill has been honored to receive select invitations to celebrated poetry events. In October 2021 Jill was a participant in a United Nations sanctioned celebration of International Non Violence Day, an annual gathering of poets on the birthday of Mahatma Gandhi. Individual poetic contributions on the shared theme of peace were compiled into an anthology, Songs of Peace. Publication credits include: Vita Brevis Press, Spillwords Press, Fine Lines, Love of Food magazine, Poetic Musings Ezine, Yasou! A Celebration Of Life Ezine, The Poet Magazine, ILA, The New York Parrot, Passion of Poetry, Patch Community News, Delaware Boots on the Ground. Jill has contributed poems and editing skills to multiple anthologies since 2018. She regularly gifts cover texts for collections of poetry. She has her own playlist on YouTube where archived are her Sparrow Productions poetry videos. The poems, Let Peace In & The Stars I'm Wishing On became the lyrics for two original songs. Jill's passions include reading aloud with her husband Tim Little, a chosen pleasure they continue, despite their frequent, forced, health related separations. She enjoys live theatre, book discussions, & photography of food & flowers. She loves cooking from the heart & is never happier than when she has a "student" in the kitchen & her imagination soars. Her love of cooking is evident throughout her poetry & in conversations. She lives in Delaware, USA with her husband Tim, & is a proud mother of her son Jordan.

TOP SEVENTY LITERARY LIONESSES OF 2022

These lovely literary lionesses were chosen for their contributions and talents to the art of literature. This recognition wishes to highlight deserving voices and workers of the mind across continents.

1. Athena Kildegaard	28. Sharon Presley
2. Sumrita Urni Ganguly	29. Shamayita Sen
3. Lisa Marie Basile	30. Suchismita Ghoshal
4. Meghan McClure	31. Zaneta Johns
5. Priyanka Banerjee	32. Saras Lysyk
6. Ngozi Olivia Osuoha	33. Joanne Penn Cooper
7. Faleeha Hassan	34. Anne Whitehouse
8. Bogdana Gageanu	35. Christine Stoddard
9. Franca Colozzo	36. Alina Stefanescu
10. Isilda Nunes	37. Kavita Ezekiel Mendonca
11. Jagari Mukherjee	38. Aliki Barnstone
12. Annette Tarpley	39. Srividya Sivakumar
13. Vatsala Radhakeesoon	40. Thasia Anne Lunger
14. Jhilam Chattaraj	41. Michela Zanarella
15. Tali Cohen Shabtai	42. Billie Duncan
16. Rachel Custer	43. Megha Sood
17. Rachael Ikins	44. Candice Louisa Daquin
18. Wang Ping	45. Melissa Chappell
19. Gili Haimovich	46. Chryssa Velissariou
20. Elina Petrova	47. Catherine Zickgraf
21. Amrita Valan	48. Lorraine Currelley
22. Elizabeth Esguerro Castillo	49. Manja Najthefer Popov
23. Inga Zhgenti	50. Debbie Tosun Kilday
24. Laksmissree Banerjee	51. Lindsey Lerman
25. Lyn Coffin	52. Carmen Bugan
26. Pramila Venjkateswaran	53. Heather Bell
27. Usha Akella	54. Vera Ikon

55. Nikita Parik

56. Mallika Bhaumik

57. Ananya Chatterjee

58. Tina Whittendorf Mortensen

59. W. Ruth Kozak

60. Emily Fortney

61. Elizabeth Ogunmodede

62. Lisa Joy Tomey

63. Carrie Kornacki

64. Anna McEnulty

65. Lidia Chiarelli

66. Eva Zelanay

67. Melissa Studdard

68. Sarah Law

69. Monalisa Parida

70. Moitreyee Raju

"JANANI"

- Priyanka Banerjee

The infant challenges the cosmos, while drinking nectar from its mother's breast.

One drop of tear engulfs

The ocean of milk -

Kissed forehead reflects

God's light !

Utterances vibrate into the distant world of voicelessness.

Expectations embrace prenatal restlessness.

Chanted mantras and the swollen womb breed one new surge -

" JANANI" !

When union is transformed into rebellion and stars break hearts -

Promises collapse into the Third Space -

Something that's intense creeps into the Soul !

" JANANI"!

When madness triumphs over the perennial sadness of the whirling planets -

Rushing particles adore the naked majesty of the dilapidated structure!

Atoms Pine for darkest, lustful atoms

That love to suffer -

Beasts howl together

Resisting the treacherous Instincts

Of feminine history

Of traumatized silence.

Bloodstained eyes

Take resort to the mythical tales

Of flaws -

The evening stars bless the Parting lovers

With solemn grandeur.

The pregnant mistress plays with moments of midnight anguish

And stolen fire !

Something still burns within the Sinking bark of absolute

Solitude -

Stars break the laws !

Your laws! My flaws!

The mother shouts out in blind anger,

Chanting words

Of birth, pain and furore -

Darkness envelops the bleeding womb Defying the century's

Ire !

Blood demands blood;

Warmth negates pain;

Deadly splits love new connections.

Stars bless the bondages of the vibrating, raging, Mysterios umbilical cords that defy pain.

Suddenly, shadows unfold the dancing worshipper's

Ancient tale

Of ceremony of love.

Rolling clouds adore the virgin's heart.

Lust and Sin forsake the earth.

Love triumphs over love

As light illuminates the naked body of rotten impulse !

The infant becomes silent again -

Midnight veil plays with veins.

"JANANI"!

Notes - "JANANI" means the Mother.

Priyanka Banerjee is a bilingual poet from Kolkata, India. She is also an Academician and she publishes her poetry in International journals like INNSAEI. Her poems got published in various International Anthologies like Paradise on Earth (Florida), Timeless Inspiration (India), Bengali English Poets (USA). She has also published poems in various Web portals of various countries like Williwashwordpress.com, The Moment International (Egypt), newyorkparrot.com (USA), Surjoday Foundation.com (India), Humayun Editorials (Bangladesh), Aksharang.com(Nepal), Sahitya Samvedanam(Bangladesh). Priyanka Banerjee is also a performance poet and her youtube channel, Priyanka Banerjee, the Poetess is appreciated all over the world. She has also recently been awarded Gujarat Sahitya Academy Award by Gujarat Sahitya Academy.

Happy Women's
Day